Practical Guidance for a Spirit-L.E.D. Life

S. A. L. T.
& D. O. E. R.

A Christian Devotional for
Life-Application, Evangelism,
and Discipleship

Practical Guidance for a Spirit-L.E.D. Life

S.A.L.T. & D.O.E.R.

A Christian Devotional for
Life-Application, Evangelism,
and Discipleship

TERIA SAMPANEY

Copyright © 2025 Teria Sampaney
All rights reserved.

No part of this book may be reproduced, stored in a retrieval system, or transmitted in any form or by any means—electronic, mechanical, photocopying, recording, or otherwise, without prior written permission of the author, except for brief quotations in reviews or articles.

Scripture quotations are taken from the Holy Bible, New Century Version.

This book is intended to provide information and inspiration for personal growth and spiritual development. The author is not liable for any misuse or misinterpretation of the content provided herein.

Published by FI NIX SIX MEDIA
Contact: www.aliciaredmond.com
ISBN: 978-1-7347318-3-5

Table of Contents

Acknowledgement   7

Foreword   9

Introduction   11

What Is This Book About?
It's a "Live-A-Long"   13

How To Use This Book   15

Sections

LOVE   19

FAMILY & RELATIONSHIPS   71

TRUST & HOPE   123

FINANCE   175

Acknowledgement

First and foremost, I give all glory and honor to God, who has been my guide, my strength, and the source of every word within these pages. Without His grace and inspiration, this devotional would not exist.

I am deeply grateful to my parents, Bernard and Donna Fields, who instilled in me a love for God's Word and a steadfast commitment to living out my faith. Your guidance, prayers, and encouragement laid the foundation for everything I am today.

To the pastors, mentors, and church community who shaped my spiritual journey, thank you for your faithful teaching, wisdom, and example. Your investment in my growth has borne fruit in ways I could never have imagined.

To everyone who has poured into my life—family, friends, and fellow believers—your love, support, and prayers have been invaluable. This devotional is a reflection of the truths you have helped me discover along the way.

May this work bring glory to God and be a blessing to all who read it.

With gratitude,
Teria Sampaney

Foreword

I am a lover of the Word of God and have spent the last 60 years striving to live out what I've read. Every one of us faces the challenge of deciding how to spend our precious time.

This easy-to-read biblical tool offers transformational rewards, showing that time spent in God's Word not only enriches our own lives but equips us to share His truth with others.

S.A.L.T. & D.O.E.R. is a devotional that will prompt you to reflect deeply on how you're living your time on this earth, guiding you toward a life of purpose and impact. It seamlessly integrates lifestyle with learning and equips believers to share the Gospel in meaningful ways. The format draws both the mind and soul into a stronger desire to live life to the fullest, not only for personal growth, but as a light to those around you.

It's not hard to imagine small groups, individuals, churches, and even online communities using this resource to connect, grow, and share the Gospel with boldness.

I'm proud to say this book is the brainchild of someone I've had the privilege of knowing for decades. The creativity within these pages speaks directly to the heart of the author—someone who has spent their life purposefully walking out their faith while diligently seeking the truth of God's Word for everyday living.

S.A.L.T. & D.O.E.R. is a powerful evangelism tool and an invitation to reflect and embed God's Word in our daily walk. It encourages us not only to live the Word but to share it... in our homes, workplaces, communities, and beyond.

So, join me. Be inspired, get creative, and share this masterpiece both in your own life and in the lives of those who need to know Him.

Donna Fields

INTRODUCTION

Busy. Work. Group chats. Deadlines. Family check-ins. Last-minute errands. Church. School. Catching up. Scrolling. Rest (if you're lucky). Side hustles. Social events. Trying to breathe.

The list goes on and on and on. But where's the time to read the Word, let alone meditate on it? And what about applying it?

The truth is, if we don't have time to read and meditate on the Word, we may not apply it in a way that's meaningful to our lives and the lives of those around us.

Shouldn't we be applying the Word in our daily interactions? Isn't that what we're called to do? Absolutely! But how do we do that in the busyness of life?

I hope this book serves as a solution to that question for you and to those around you.

WHAT IS THIS BOOK ABOUT?
It's a "Live-A-Long"

This isn't a daily check-the-box devotional. It's what I call a "live-a-long." Instead of simply reading a verse and moving on, you'll be invited to:

- Reflect on Scripture.

- Respond with personal insight.

- Live it out in everyday interactions with family, friends, and your community.

Each section is designed to bridge the gap between reading God's Word and living God's Word. Think of it as a guide to help you weave faith into the everyday rhythms of life. Whether you're waiting in the carpool line, gathered around the dinner table, in late-night talks with friends, or facing the small choices that shape your day, this book will serve as a gentle companion and reminder that faith isn't confined to quiet moments... it's lived out in real ones.

HOW TO USE THIS BOOK

S.A.L.T. & D.O.E.R. is based on two foundational scriptures:

Matthew 5:13
Ye are the salt of the earth…
and
James 1:22
But be ye doers of the word, and not hearers only,…

The book is divided into four sections: Love, Family and Relationships, Trust and Hope, and Finance. You may begin with whichever section you feel led to explore. Each section contains twelve Focus Scriptures, paired with the guiding acronyms S.A.L.T. and D.O.E.R. To help you track your journey, the scriptures are numbered in the top corners (e.g., *S.A.L.T. 1 and D.O.E.R. 1* through *48*), so you'll always know where you are.

HOW TO USE THE ACRONYMS

The acronyms invite you to reflect on two key questions:

1. How can I be **salt** in my public life?
2. How can I be a **doer** in my private life?

Each letter in both acronyms presents a question for you to meditate on. As you reflect, consider how to put each one into action in your public and private life.

S.A.L.T.

- ***S.*** — *How can I **SHOW** others?*
- ***A.*** — *How can I **ACKNOWLEDGE** this scripture in the actions of others?*
- ***L.*** — *What can I **LISTEN** for during conversation?*
- ***T.*** — *What can I **TELL** others about this scripture?*

D.O.E.R.

- ***D.*** — *What can I **DO** to live out this scripture?*
- ***O.*** — *What **OPPORTUNITY** do I see to live out this scripture?*
- ***E.*** — *How can I **EXPRESS** myself with this scripture?*
- ***R.*** — *How can I **RECOGNIZE** this scripture in others?*

How often should I use it?

There's no one way to use this book. You can focus on the application of one scripture per week or you can use it bi-weekly, or even monthly. It's completely up to you!

Can I use this alone?

Sure! This book can be used individually or with family and friends. If you're using it with others, be sure each person has their own copy to make notes along the way.

What do I do with it?

Read the Focus Scripture. Then, reflect and make notes on how you can live as S.A.L.T. in light of that verse. Next, write down how you can be a D.O.E.R. of the word. Finally, put it into practice. Live it out in your daily interactions with those around you.

PRAYER

Heavenly Father,

Thank You for the privilege of sharing Your Word with others. I lift up every person reading this book, asking that they encounter You in a deeply personal and transformative way. May Your truth speak directly to their hearts, blessing not only their own lives but also those they touch.

Lord, help us to see Your Word as a living guide, practical, powerful, and relevant for every moment of our lives. Teach us to apply its wisdom in how we think, act, and engage with others.

I pray for open doors to share Your Word in the future, inspired by the seeds planted through this book. Let the insights we gain illuminate our paths, enrich our lives, and equip us to be lights in the lives of others, drawing them closer to You.

We praise You for the gift of Your Word. It's a steadfast guide and source of strength in every season. May it shape us to reflect Your love and purpose daily.

In Jesus' Name, Amen.

LOVE

1 Corinthians 13:4
Charity suffereth long, and is kind; charity envieth not; charity vaunteth not itself, is not puffed up,...

How can I be S.A.L.T. in my public life?

S. <u>How can I SHOW others?</u>

A. <u>How can I ACKNOWLEDGE this scripture in the actions of others?</u>

L. **What can I LISTEN for during conversation?**

T. **What can I TELL others about this scripture?**

1 Corinthians 13:4

Charity suffereth long, and is kind; charity envieth not; charity vaunteth not itself, is not puffed up,...

How can I be a D.O.E.R. in my private life?

D. <u>What can I DO to live out this scripture?</u>

O. <u>What OPPORTUNITY do I see to live out this scripture?</u>

D.O.E.R. 1

E. <u>How can I EXPRESS myself with this scripture?</u>

R. <u>How can I RECOGNIZE this scripture in others?</u>

Romans 12:10
Love each other with genuine affection,
and take delight in honoring each other.

How can I be S.A.L.T. in my public life?

S. How can I SHOW others?

A. How can I ACKNOWLEDGE this scripture in the actions of others?

L. <u>What can I LISTEN for during conversation?</u>

T. <u>What can I TELL others about this scripture?</u>

Romans 12:10
*Love each other with genuine affection,
and take delight in honoring each other.*

How can I be a D.O.E.R. in my private life?

D. <u>**What can I DO to live out this scripture?**</u>

O. <u>**What OPPORTUNITY do I see to live out this scripture?**</u>

E. How can I EXPRESS myself with this scripture?

R. How can I RECOGNIZE this scripture in others?

1 Corinthians 13:7
Love is always supportive, loyal, hopeful, and trusting.

How can I be S.A.L.T. in my public life?

S. <u>How can I SHOW others?</u>

A. <u>How can I ACKNOWLEDGE this scripture in the actions of others?</u>

L. What can I LISTEN for during conversation?

T. What can I TELL others about this scripture?

1 Corinthians 13:7
Love is always supportive, loyal, hopeful, and trusting.

How can I be a D.O.E.R. in my private life?

D. <u>What can I DO to live out this scripture?</u>

O. <u>What OPPORTUNITY do I see to live out this scripture?</u>

E. How can I EXPRESS myself with this scripture?

R. How can I RECOGNIZE this scripture in others?

Colossians 3:14
*Do all these things; but most important, love each other.
Love is what holds you all together in perfect unity.*

How can I be S.A.L.T. in my public life?

S. <u>How can I SHOW others?</u>

A. <u>How can I ACKNOWLEDGE this scripture in the actions of others?</u>

L. What can I LISTEN for during conversation?

T. What can I TELL others about this scripture?

Colossians 3:14
Do all these things; but most important, love each other.
Love is what holds you all together in perfect unity.

How can I be a D.O.E.R. in my private life?

D. <u>**What can I DO to live out this scripture?**</u>

O. <u>**What OPPORTUNITY do I see to live out this scripture?**</u>

E. How can I EXPRESS myself with this scripture?

R. How can I RECOGNIZE this scripture in others?

1 Peter 4:8
Most importantly, love each other deeply,
because love will cause many sins to be forgiven.

How can I be S.A.L.T. in my public life?

S. <u>How can I SHOW others?</u>

A. <u>How can I ACKNOWLEDGE this scripture in the actions of others?</u>

L. What can I LISTEN for during conversation?

T. What can I TELL others about this scripture?

1 Peter 4:8
*Most importantly, love each other deeply,
because love will cause many sins to be forgiven.*

How can I be a D.O.E.R. in my private life?

D. <u>**What can I DO to live out this scripture?**</u>

O. <u>**What OPPORTUNITY do I see to live out this scripture?**</u>

E. How can I EXPRESS myself with this scripture?

R. How can I RECOGNIZE this scripture in others?

1 Corinthians 16:14
Do everything in love.

How can I be S.A.L.T. in my public life?

S. <u>How can I SHOW others?</u>

A. <u>How can I ACKNOWLEDGE this scripture in the actions of others?</u>

L. <u>What can I LISTEN for during conversation?</u>

T. <u>What can I TELL others about this scripture?</u>

1 Corinthians 16:14
Do everything in love.

How can I be a D.O.E.R. in my private life?

D. <u>What can I DO to live out this scripture?</u>

O. <u>What OPPORTUNITY do I see to live out this scripture?</u>

D.O.E.R. 6

E. How can I EXPRESS myself with this scripture?

R. How can I RECOGNIZE this scripture in others?

Proverbs 10:12
Hatred stirs up trouble, but love forgives all wrongs.

How can I be S.A.L.T. in my public life?

S. How can I SHOW others?

A. How can I ACKNOWLEDGE this scripture in the actions of others?

L. What can I LISTEN for during conversation?

T. What can I TELL others about this scripture?

Proverbs 10:12
Hatred stirs up trouble, but love forgives all wrongs.

How can I be a D.O.E.R. in my private life?

D. <u>What can I DO to live out this scripture?</u>

O. <u>What OPPORTUNITY do I see to live out this scripture?</u>

E. <u>How can I EXPRESS myself with this scripture?</u>

R. <u>How can I RECOGNIZE this scripture in others?</u>

Romans 9:10
*Your love must be real. Hate what is evil,
and hold on to what is good.*

How can I be S.A.L.T. in my public life?

S. <u>How can I SHOW others?</u>

A. <u>How can I ACKNOWLEDGE this scripture in the actions of others?</u>

L. What can I LISTEN for during conversation?

T. What can I TELL others about this scripture?

Romans 9:10
*Your love must be real. Hate what is evil,
and hold on to what is good.*

How can I be a D.O.E.R. in my private life?

D. <u>**What can I DO to live out this scripture?**</u>

O. <u>**What OPPORTUNITY do I see to live out this scripture?**</u>

E. How can I EXPRESS myself with this scripture?

R. How can I RECOGNIZE this scripture in others?

Romans 13:8

Do not owe people anything, except always owe love to each other, because the person who loves others has obeyed all the law.

How can I be S.A.L.T. in my public life?

S. How can I SHOW others?

A. How can I ACKNOWLEDGE this scripture in the actions of others?

L. **What can I LISTEN for during conversation?**

T. **What can I TELL others about this scripture?**

Romans 13:8
Do not owe people anything, except always owe love to each other, because the person who loves others has obeyed all the law.

How can I be a D.O.E.R. in my private life?

D. <u>**What can I DO to live out this scripture?**</u>

O. <u>**What OPPORTUNITY do I see to live out this scripture?**</u>

E. How can I EXPRESS myself with this scripture?

R. How can I RECOGNIZE this scripture in others?

Romans 13:10
*Love never hurts a neighbor,
so loving is obeying all the law.*

How can I be S.A.L.T. in my public life?

S. How can I SHOW others?

A. How can I ACKNOWLEDGE this scripture in the actions of others?

L. <u>What can I LISTEN for during conversation?</u>

T. <u>What can I TELL others about this scripture?</u>

Romans 13:10
*Love never hurts a neighbor,
so loving is obeying all the law.*

How can I be a D.O.E.R. in my private life?

D. **What can I DO to live out this scripture?**

O. **What OPPORTUNITY do I see to live out this scripture?**

E. How can I EXPRESS myself with this scripture?

R. How can I RECOGNIZE this scripture in others?

Luke 6:27
*But I say to you who are listening, love your enemies.
Do good to those who hate you...*

How can I be S.A.L.T. in my public life?

S. <u>How can I SHOW others?</u>

A. <u>How can I ACKNOWLEDGE this scripture in the actions of others?</u>

S.A.L.T. 11

L. What can I LISTEN for during conversation?

T. What can I TELL others about this scripture?

Luke 6:27
*But I say to you who are listening, love your enemies.
Do good to those who hate you...*

How can I be a D.O.E.R. in my private life?

D. <u>**What can I DO to live out this scripture?**</u>

O. <u>**What OPPORTUNITY do I see to live out this scripture?**</u>

E. How can I EXPRESS myself with this scripture?

R. How can I RECOGNIZE this scripture in others?

1 Corinthians 13:13
So these three things continue forever: faith, hope, and love. And the greatest of these is love.

How can I be S.A.L.T. in my public life?

S. How can I SHOW others?

A. How can I ACKNOWLEDGE this scripture in the actions of others?

L. <u>What can I LISTEN for during conversation?</u>

T. <u>What can I TELL others about this scripture?</u>

1 Corinthians 13:13
So these three things continue forever: faith, hope, and love. And the greatest of these is love.

How can I be a D.O.E.R. in my private life?

D. <u>**What can I DO to live out this scripture?**</u>

O. <u>**What OPPORTUNITY do I see to live out this scripture?**</u>

D.O.E.R. 12

E. How can I EXPRESS myself with this scripture?

R. How can I RECOGNIZE this scripture in others?

FAMILY & RELATIONSHIPS

Romans 12:18
Do your best to live in peace with everyone.

How can I be S.A.L.T. in my public life?

S. <u>How can I SHOW others?</u>

A. <u>How can I ACKNOWLEDGE this scripture in the actions of others?</u>

L. **What can I LISTEN for during conversation?**

T. **What can I TELL others about this scripture?**

Romans 12:18
Do your best to live in peace with everyone.

How can I be a D.O.E.R. in my private life?

D. <u>**What can I DO to live out this scripture?**</u>

O. <u>**What OPPORTUNITY do I see to live out this scripture?**</u>

D.O.E.R. 13

E. How can I EXPRESS myself with this scripture?

R. How can I RECOGNIZE this scripture in others?

Proverbs 18:24
*Some friends may ruin you,
but a real friend will be more loyal than a brother.*

How can I be S.A.L.T. in my public life?

S. <u>How can I SHOW others?</u>

A. <u>How can I ACKNOWLEDGE this scripture in the actions of others?</u>

L. What can I LISTEN for during conversation?

T. What can I TELL others about this scripture?

Proverbs 18:24
*Some friends may ruin you,
but a real friend will be more loyal than a brother.*

How can I be a D.O.E.R. in my private life?

D. <u>**What can I DO to live out this scripture?**</u>

O. <u>**What OPPORTUNITY do I see to live out this scripture?**</u>

E. How can I EXPRESS myself with this scripture?

R. How can I RECOGNIZE this scripture in others?

Phillippians 2:3
When you do things, do not let selfishness or pride be your guide. Instead, be humble and give more honor to others than to yourselves.

How can I be S.A.L.T. in my public life?

S. **How can I SHOW others?**

A. **How can I ACKNOWLEDGE this scripture in the actions of others?**

L. What can I LISTEN for during conversation?

T. What can I TELL others about this scripture?

Phillippians 2:3
When you do things, do not let selfishness or pride be your guide. Instead, be humble and give more honor to others than to yourselves.

How can I be a D.O.E.R. in my private life?

D. <u>**What can I DO to live out this scripture?**</u>

O. <u>**What OPPORTUNITY do I see to live out this scripture?**</u>

E. <u>How can I EXPRESS myself with this scripture?</u>

R. <u>How can I RECOGNIZE this scripture in others?</u>

Proverbs 27:17
As iron sharpens iron, so people can improve each other.

How can I be S.A.L.T. in my public life?

S. How can I SHOW others?

A. How can I ACKNOWLEDGE this scripture in the actions of others?

L. <u>What can I LISTEN for during conversation?</u>

T. <u>What can I TELL others about this scripture?</u>

Proverbs 27:17
As iron sharpens iron, so people can improve each other.

How can I be a D.O.E.R. in my private life?

D. <u>What can I DO to live out this scripture?</u>

O. <u>What OPPORTUNITY do I see to live out this scripture?</u>

D.O.E.R. 16

E. How can I EXPRESS myself with this scripture?

R. How can I RECOGNIZE this scripture in others?

Phillippians 2:4
*Do not be interested only in your own life,
but be interested in the lives of others.*

How can I be S.A.L.T. in my public life?

S. <u>How can I SHOW others?</u>

A. <u>How can I ACKNOWLEDGE this scripture in the actions of others?</u>

L. <u>What can I LISTEN for during conversation?</u>

T. <u>What can I TELL others about this scripture?</u>

Phillippians 2:4
*Do not be interested only in your own life,
but be interested in the lives of others.*

How can I be a D.O.E.R. in my private life?

D. <u>What can I DO to live out this scripture?</u>

O. <u>What OPPORTUNITY do I see to live out this scripture?</u>

E. How can I EXPRESS myself with this scripture?

R. How can I RECOGNIZE this scripture in others?

Proverbs 17:17
*A friend loves you all the time,
and a brother helps in time of trouble.*

How can I be S.A.L.T. in my public life?

S. How can I SHOW others?

A. How can I ACKNOWLEDGE this scripture in the actions of others?

L. What can I LISTEN for during conversation?

T. What can I TELL others about this scripture?

Proverbs 17:17
*A friend loves you all the time,
and a brother helps in time of trouble.*

How can I be a D.O.E.R. in my private life?

D. <u>What can I DO to live out this scripture?</u>

O. <u>What OPPORTUNITY do I see to live out this scripture?</u>

E. How can I EXPRESS myself with this scripture?

R. How can I RECOGNIZE this scripture in others?

Galatians 6:9
Don't get tired of helping others. You will be rewarded when the time is right, if you don't give up.

How can I be S.A.L.T. in my public life?

S. <u>How can I SHOW others?</u>

A. <u>How can I ACKNOWLEDGE this scripture in the actions of others?</u>

L. <u>What can I LISTEN for during conversation?</u>

T. <u>What can I TELL others about this scripture?</u>

Galatians 6:9
Don't get tired of helping others. You will be rewarded when the time is right, if you don't give up.

How can I be a D.O.E.R. in my private life?

D. <u>What can I DO to live out this scripture?</u>

O. <u>What **OPPORTUNITY** do I see to live out this scripture?</u>

E. How can I EXPRESS myself with this scripture?

R. How can I RECOGNIZE this scripture in others?

Proverbs 13:20
*Walk with the wise and become wise;
associate with fools and get in trouble.*

How can I be S.A.L.T. in my public life?

S. <u>How can I SHOW others?</u>

A. <u>How can I ACKNOWLEDGE this scripture in the actions of others?</u>

S.A.L.T. 20

L. **What can I LISTEN for during conversation?**

T. **What can I TELL others about this scripture?**

Proverbs 13:20
*Walk with the wise and become wise;
associate with fools and get in trouble.*

How can I be a D.O.E.R. in my private life?

D. <u>What can I DO to live out this scripture?</u>

O. <u>What OPPORTUNITY do I see to live out this scripture?</u>

E. How can I EXPRESS myself with this scripture?

R. How can I RECOGNIZE this scripture in others?

Proverbs 27:6
Wounds from a sincere friend are better than many kisses from an enemy.

How can I be S.A.L.T. in my public life?

S. <u>How can I SHOW others?</u>

A. <u>How can I ACKNOWLEDGE this scripture in the actions of others?</u>

L. What can I LISTEN for during conversation?

T. What can I TELL others about this scripture?

Proverbs 27:6
Wounds from a sincere friend are better than many kisses from an enemy.

How can I be a D.O.E.R. in my private life?

D. <u>**What can I DO to live out this scripture?**</u>

O. <u>**What OPPORTUNITY do I see to live out this scripture?**</u>

E. <u>How can I EXPRESS myself with this scripture?</u>

R. <u>How can I RECOGNIZE this scripture in others?</u>

Ephesians 4:2
Always be humble and gentle.
Patiently put up with each other and love each other.

How can I be S.A.L.T. in my public life?

S. <u>How can I SHOW others?</u>

A. <u>How can I ACKNOWLEDGE this scripture in the actions of others?</u>

S.A.L.T. 22

L. **What can I LISTEN for during conversation?**

T. **What can I TELL others about this scripture?**

Ephesians 4:2
*Always be humble and gentle.
Patiently put up with each other and love each other.*

How can I be a D.O.E.R. in my private life?

D. <u>What can I DO to live out this scripture?</u>

O. <u>What OPPORTUNITY do I see to live out this scripture?</u>

E. How can I EXPRESS myself with this scripture?

R. How can I RECOGNIZE this scripture in others?

Ecclesiastes 4:9
*Two people are better off than one,
for they can help each other succeed.*

How can I be S.A.L.T. in my public life?

S. **How can I SHOW others?**

A. **How can I ACKNOWLEDGE this scripture in the actions of others?**

L. <u>What can I LISTEN for during conversation?</u>

T. <u>What can I TELL others about this scripture?</u>

Ecclesiastes 4:9
*Two people are better off than one,
for they can help each other succeed.*

How can I be a D.O.E.R. in my private life?

D. <u>What can I DO to live out this scripture?</u>

O. <u>What OPPORTUNITY do I see to live out this scripture?</u>

E. How can I EXPRESS myself with this scripture?

R. How can I RECOGNIZE this scripture in others?

Luke 6:37

Don't judge others, and God won't judge you.
Don't be hard on others, and God won't be hard on you.
Forgive others, and God will forgive you.

How can I be S.A.L.T. in my public life?

S. <u>How can I SHOW others?</u>

A. <u>How can I ACKNOWLEDGE this scripture in the actions of others?</u>

L. **What can I LISTEN for during conversation?**

T. **What can I TELL others about this scripture?**

Luke 6:37
Don't judge others, and God won't judge you.
Don't be hard on others, and God won't be hard on you.
Forgive others, and God will forgive you.

How can I be a D.O.E.R. in my private life?

D. <u>**What can I DO to live out this scripture?**</u>

O. <u>**What OPPORTUNITY do I see to live out this scripture?**</u>

D.O.E.R. 24

E. How can I EXPRESS myself with this scripture?

R. How can I RECOGNIZE this scripture in others?

TRUST & HOPE

Proverbs 3:5
*Trust the Lord with all your heart,
and don't depend on your own understanding.*

How can I be S.A.L.T. in my public life?

S. How can I SHOW others?

A. How can I ACKNOWLEDGE this scripture in the actions of others?

L. What can I LISTEN for during conversation?

T. What can I TELL others about this scripture?

Proverbs 3:5
*Trust the Lord with all your heart,
and don't depend on your own understanding.*

How can I be a D.O.E.R. in my private life?

D. **What can I DO to live out this scripture?**

O. **What OPPORTUNITY do I see to live out this scripture?**

E. How can I EXPRESS myself with this scripture?

R. How can I RECOGNIZE this scripture in others?

Jeremiah 29:11

I say this because I know what I am planning for you," says the Lord. "I have good plans for you, not plans to hurt you. I will give you hope and a good future.

How can I be S.A.L.T. in my public life?

S. How can I SHOW others?

A. How can I ACKNOWLEDGE this scripture in the actions of others?

L. <u>What can I LISTEN for during conversation?</u>

T. <u>What can I TELL others about this scripture?</u>

Jeremiah 29:11

*I say this because I know what I am planning for you," says the Lord. "I have good plans for you, not plans to hurt you.
I will give you hope and a good future.*

How can I be a D.O.E.R. in my public life?

D. <u>What can I DO to live out this scripture?</u>

O. <u>What OPPORTUNITY do I see to live out this scripture?</u>

D.O.E.R. 26

E. <u>How can I EXPRESS myself with this scripture?</u>

R. <u>How can I RECOGNIZE this scripture in others?</u>

Hebrews 11:1
Faith means being sure of the things we hope for and knowing that something is real even if we do not see it.

How can I be S.A.L.T. in my public life?

S. <u>How can I SHOW others?</u>

A. <u>How can I ACKNOWLEDGE this scripture in the actions of others?</u>

S.A.L.T. 27

L. <u>What can I LISTEN for during conversation?</u>

T. <u>What can I TELL others about this scripture?</u>

Hebrews 11:1
Faith means being sure of the things we hope for and knowing that something is real even if we do not see it.

How can I be a D.O.E.R. in my private life?

D. <u>What can I DO to live out this scripture?</u>

O. <u>What OPPORTUNITY do I see to live out this scripture?</u>

E. How can I EXPRESS myself with this scripture?

R. How can I RECOGNIZE this scripture in others?

Joshua 1:9
Remember that I commanded you to be strong and brave. Don't be afraid...

How can I be S.A.L.T. in my public life?

S. How can I SHOW others?

A. How can I ACKNOWLEDGE this scripture in the actions of others?

S.A.L.T. 28

L. <u>What can I LISTEN for during conversation?</u>

T. <u>What can I TELL others about this scripture?</u>

Joshua 1:9
Remember that I commanded you to be strong and brave. Don't be afraid...

How can I be a D.O.E.R. in my private life?

D. <u>What can I DO to live out this scripture?</u>

O. <u>What OPPORTUNITY do I see to live out this scripture?</u>

E. How can I EXPRESS myself with this scripture?

R. How can I RECOGNIZE this scripture in others?

1 Corinthians 13:4
So I tell you, don't worry about the food or drink you need to live, or about the clothes you need for your body. Life is more than food, and the body is more than clothes.

How can I be S.A.L.T. in my public life?

S. How can I SHOW others?

A. How can I ACKNOWLEDGE this scripture in the actions of others?

L. What can I LISTEN for during conversation?

T. What can I TELL others about this scripture?

1 Corinthians 13:4

So I tell you, don't worry about the food or drink you need to live, or about the clothes you need for your body. Life is more than food, and the body is more than clothes.

How can I be a D.O.E.R. in my private life?

D. **What can I DO to live out this scripture?**

O. **What OPPORTUNITY do I see to live out this scripture?**

E. <u>How can I EXPRESS myself with this scripture?</u>

R. <u>How can I RECOGNIZE this scripture in others?</u>

John 14:1
Don't let your hearts be troubled.

How can I be S.A.L.T. in my public life?

S. **How can I SHOW others?**

A. **How can I ACKNOWLEDGE this scripture in the actions of others?**

L. <u>What can I LISTEN for during conversation?</u>

T. <u>What can I TELL others about this scripture?</u>

John 14:1
Don't let your hearts be troubled.

How can I be a D.O.E.R. in my private life?

D. <u>What can I DO to live out this scripture?</u>

O. <u>What OPPORTUNITY do I see to live out this scripture?</u>

E. How can I EXPRESS myself with this scripture?

R. How can I RECOGNIZE this scripture in others?

Romans 5:3 - 4

We also have joy with our troubles, because we know that these troubles produce patience. And patience produces character, and character produces hope.

How can I be S.A.L.T. in my public life?

S. How can I SHOW others?

A. How can I ACKNOWLEDGE this scripture in the actions of others?

S.A.L.T. 31

L. <u>What can I LISTEN for during conversation?</u>

T. <u>What can I TELL others about this scripture?</u>

Romans 5:3 - 4

We also have joy with our troubles, because we know that these troubles produce patience. And patience produces character, and character produces hope.

How can I be a D.O.E.R. in my private life?

D. <u>**What can I DO to live out this scripture?**</u>

O. <u>**What OPPORTUNITY do I see to live out this scripture?**</u>

E. <u>How can I EXPRESS myself with this scripture?</u>

R. <u>How can I RECOGNIZE this scripture in others?</u>

Romans 8:24 - 25

...If we see what we are waiting for, that is not really hope. People do not hope for something they already have. But we are hoping for something we do not have yet, and we are waiting for it patiently.

How can I be S.A.L.T. in my public life?

S. **How can I SHOW others?**

A. **How can I ACKNOWLEDGE this scripture in the actions of others?**

S.A.L.T. 32

L. What can I LISTEN for during conversation?

T. What can I TELL others about this scripture?

Romans 8:24 - 25

...If we see what we are waiting for, that is not really hope. People do not hope for something they already have. But we are hoping for something we do not have yet, and we are waiting for it patiently.

How can I be a D.O.E.R. in my private life?

D. <u>**What can I DO to live out this scripture?**</u>

O. <u>**What OPPORTUNITY do I see to live out this scripture?**</u>

E. <u>How can I EXPRESS myself with this scripture?</u>

R. <u>How can I RECOGNIZE this scripture in others?</u>

Romans 12:12

Be joyful because you have hope.
Be patient when trouble comes, and pray at all times.

How can I be S.A.L.T. in my public life?

S. How can I SHOW others?

A. How can I ACKNOWLEDGE this scripture in the actions of others?

S.A.L.T. 33

L. <u>What can I LISTEN for during conversation?</u>

T. <u>What can I TELL others about this scripture?</u>

Romans 12:12
Be joyful because you have hope.
Be patient when trouble comes, and pray at all times.

How can I be a D.O.E.R. in my private life?

D. <u>What can I DO to live out this scripture?</u>

O. <u>What OPPORTUNITY do I see to live out this scripture?</u>

D.O.E.R. 33

E. How can I EXPRESS myself with this scripture?

R. How can I RECOGNIZE this scripture in others?

Mark 9:23
...All things are possible for the one who believes.

How can I be S.A.L.T. in my public life?

S. <u>**How can I SHOW others?**</u>

A. <u>**How can I ACKNOWLEDGE this scripture in the actions of others?**</u>

L. <u>What can I LISTEN for during conversation?</u>

T. <u>What can I TELL others about this scripture?</u>

Mark 9:23
...All things are possible for the one who believes.

How can I be a D.O.E.R. in my public life?

D. <u>What can I DO to live out this scripture?</u>

O. <u>What OPPORTUNITY do I see to live out this scripture?</u>

D.O.E.R. 34

E. How can I EXPRESS myself with this scripture?

R. How can I RECOGNIZE this scripture in others?

Psalm 9:18
But those who have troubles will not be forgotten.
The hopes of the poor will never die.

How can I be S.A.L.T. in my public life?

S. <u>How can I SHOW others?</u>

A. <u>How can I ACKNOWLEDGE this scripture in the actions of others?</u>

S.A.L.T. 35

L. What can I LISTEN for during conversation?

T. What can I TELL others about this scripture?

Psalm 9:18
But those who have troubles will not be forgotten.
The hopes of the poor will never die.

How can I be a D.O.E.R. in my private life?

D. <u>What can I DO to live out this scripture?</u>

O. <u>What OPPORTUNITY do I see to live out this scripture?</u>

D.O.E.R. 35

E. How can I EXPRESS myself with this scripture?

R. How can I RECOGNIZE this scripture in others?

Psalm 46:1
God is our protection and our strength.
He always helps in times of trouble.

How can I be S.A.L.T. in my public life?

S. How can I SHOW others?

A. How can I ACKNOWLEDGE this scripture in the actions of others?

S.A.L.T. 36

L. <u>What can I LISTEN for during conversation?</u>

T. <u>What can I TELL others about this scripture?</u>

Psalm 46:1
*God is our protection and our strength.
He always helps in times of trouble.*

How can I be a D.O.E.R. in my private life?

D. <u>What can I DO to live out this scripture?</u>

O. <u>What OPPORTUNITY do I see to live out this scripture?</u>

D.O.E.R. 36

E. How can I EXPRESS myself with this scripture?

R. How can I RECOGNIZE this scripture in others?

FINANCE

Hebrews 13:5
*Keep your lives free from the love of money,
and be satisfied with what you have.*

How can I be S.A.L.T. in my public life?

S. How can I SHOW others?

A. How can I ACKNOWLEDGE this scripture in the actions of others?

S.A.L.T. 37

L. <u>What can I LISTEN for during conversation?</u>

T. <u>What can I TELL others about this scripture?</u>

Hebrews 13:5
*Keep your lives free from the love of money,
and be satisfied with what you have.*

How can I be a D.O.E.R. in my private life?

D. <u>**What can I DO to live out this scripture?**</u>

O. <u>**What OPPORTUNITY do I see to live out this scripture?**</u>

D.O.E.R. 37

E. How can I EXPRESS myself with this scripture?

R. How can I RECOGNIZE this scripture in others?

Proverbs 13:11
*Money that comes easily disappears quickly,
but money that is gathered little by little will grow.*

How can I be S.A.L.T. in my public life?

S. <u>How can I SHOW others?</u>

A. <u>How can I ACKNOWLEDGE this scripture in the actions of others?</u>

S.A.L.T. 38

L. What can I LISTEN for during conversation?

T. What can I TELL others about this scripture?

Proverbs 13:11
*Money that comes easily disappears quickly,
but money that is gathered little by little will grow.*

How can I be a D.O.E.R. in my private life?

D. <u>What can I DO to live out this scripture?</u>

O. <u>What OPPORTUNITY do I see to live out this scripture?</u>

E. How can I EXPRESS myself with this scripture?

R. How can I RECOGNIZE this scripture in others?

Luke 12:15
...Be careful and guard against all kinds of greed.
Life is not measured by how much one owns.

How can I be S.A.L.T. in my public life?

S. <u>How can I SHOW others?</u>

A. <u>How can I ACKNOWLEDGE this scripture in the actions of others?</u>

L. <u>What can I LISTEN for during conversation?</u>

T. <u>What can I TELL others about this scripture?</u>

Luke 12:15
*...Be careful and guard against all kinds of greed.
Life is not measured by how much one owns.*

How can I be a D.O.E.R. in my private life?

D. <u>What can I DO to live out this scripture?</u>

O. <u>What OPPORTUNITY do I see to live out this scripture?</u>

E. <u>How can I EXPRESS myself with this scripture?</u>

R. <u>How can I RECOGNIZE this scripture in others?</u>

Ecclesiastes 5:10
Whoever loves money will never have enough money;
Whoever loves wealth will not be satisfied with it. This is also useless.

How can I be S.A.L.T. in my public life?

S. How can I SHOW others?

A. How can I ACKNOWLEDGE this scripture in the actions of others?

L. <u>What can I LISTEN for during conversation?</u>

T. <u>What can I TELL others about this scripture?</u>

Ecclesiastes 5:10
Whoever loves money will never have enough money;
Whoever loves wealth will not be satisfied with it. This is also useless.

How can I be a D.O.E.R. in my private life?

D. <u>**What can I DO to live out this scripture?**</u>

O. <u>**What OPPORTUNITY do I see to live out this scripture?**</u>

E. How can I EXPRESS myself with this scripture?

R. How can I RECOGNIZE this scripture in others?

Matthew 6:21
Your heart will be where your treasure is.

How can I be S.A.L.T. in my public life?

S. <u>**How can I SHOW others?**</u>

A. <u>**How can I ACKNOWLEDGE this scripture in the actions of others?**</u>

L. <u>What can I LISTEN for during conversation?</u>

T. <u>What can I TELL others about this scripture?</u>

Matthew 6:21
Your heart will be where your treasure is.

How can I be a D.O.E.R. in my private life?

D. <u>**What can I DO to live out this scripture?**</u>

O. <u>**What OPPORTUNITY do I see to live out this scripture?**</u>

E. <u>How can I EXPRESS myself with this scripture?</u>

R. <u>How can I RECOGNIZE this scripture in others?</u>

Psalm 37:16
*It is better to have little and be right
than to have much and be wrong.*

How can I be S.A.L.T. in my public life?

S. <u>How can I SHOW others?</u>

A. <u>How can I ACKNOWLEDGE this scripture in the actions of others?</u>

L. What can I LISTEN for during conversation?

T. What can I TELL others about this scripture?

Psalm 37:16
*It is better to have little and be right
than to have much and be wrong.*

How can I be a D.O.E.R. in my private life?

D. <u>What can I DO to live out this scripture?</u>

O. <u>What OPPORTUNITY do I see to live out this scripture?</u>

D.O.E.R. 42

E. How can I EXPRESS myself with this scripture?

R. How can I RECOGNIZE this scripture in others?

Exodus 22:25

If you lend money to one of my people who is poor, do not treat him as a moneylender would. Charge him nothing for using your money.

How can I be S.A.L.T. in my public life?

S. How can I SHOW others?

A. How can I ACKNOWLEDGE this scripture in the actions of others?

L. <u>What can I LISTEN for during conversation?</u>

T. <u>What can I TELL others about this scripture?</u>

Exodus 22:25

If you lend money to one of my people who is poor, do not treat him as a moneylender would. Charge him nothing for using your money.

How can I be a D.O.E.R. in my private life?

D. <u>What can I DO to live out this scripture?</u>

O. <u>What OPPORTUNITY do I see to live out this scripture?</u>

D.O.E.R. 43

E. How can I EXPRESS myself with this scripture?

R. How can I RECOGNIZE this scripture in others?

1 Timothy 6:10

The love of money causes all kinds of evil. Some people have left the faith, because they wanted to get more money, but they have caused themselves much sorrow.

How can I be S.A.L.T. in my public life?

S. <u>How can I SHOW others?</u>

A. <u>How can I ACKNOWLEDGE this scripture in the actions of others?</u>

S.A.L.T. 44

L. <u>What can I LISTEN for during conversation?</u>

T. <u>What can I TELL others about this scripture?</u>

1 Timothy 6:10
The love of money causes all kinds of evil. Some people have left the faith, because they wanted to get more money, but they have caused themselves much sorrow.

How can I be a D.O.E.R. in my private life?

D. **What can I DO to live out this scripture?**

O. **What OPPORTUNITY do I see to live out this scripture?**

E. How can I EXPRESS myself with this scripture?

R. How can I RECOGNIZE this scripture in others?

1 Timothy 6:17
Command those who are rich with things of this world not to be proud...

How can I be S.A.L.T. in my public life?

S. <u>How can I SHOW others?</u>

A. <u>How can I ACKNOWLEDGE this scripture in the actions of others?</u>

S.A.L.T. 45

L. <u>What can I LISTEN for during conversation?</u>

T. <u>What can I TELL others about this scripture?</u>

1 Timothy 6:17
Command those who are rich with things of this world not to be proud...

How can I be a D.O.E.R. in my private life?

D. What can I DO to live out this scripture?

O. What OPPORTUNITY do I see to live out this scripture?

D.O.E.R. 45

E. How can I EXPRESS myself with this scripture?

R. How can I RECOGNIZE this scripture in others?

Matthew 6:3 - 4
So when you give to the poor, don't let anyone know what you are doing. Your giving should be done in secret. Your Father can see what is done in secret, and he will reward you.

How can I be S.A.L.T. in my public life?

S. <u>How can I SHOW others?</u>

A. <u>How can I ACKNOWLEDGE this scripture in the actions of others?</u>

L. <u>What can I LISTEN for during conversation?</u>

T. <u>What can I TELL others about this scripture?</u>

Matthew 6:3 - 4

So when you give to the poor, don't let anyone know what you are doing. Your giving should be done in secret. Your Father can see what is done in secret, and he will reward you.

How can I be a D.O.E.R. in my private life?

D. <u>What can I DO to live out this scripture?</u>

O. <u>What OPPORTUNITY do I see to live out this scripture?</u>

D.O.E.R. 46

E. How can I EXPRESS myself with this scripture?

R. How can I RECOGNIZE this scripture in others?

Luke 14:28
If you want to build a tower, you first sit down and decide how much it will cost, to see if you have enough money to finish the job.

How can I be S.A.L.T. in my public life?

S. How can I SHOW others?

A. How can I ACKNOWLEDGE this scripture in the actions of others?

L. **What can I LISTEN for during conversation?**

T. **What can I TELL others about this scripture?**

Luke 14:28
If you want to build a tower, you first sit down and decide how much it will cost, to see if you have enough money to finish the job.

How can I be a D.O.E.R. in my private life?

D. <u>What can I DO to live out this scripture?</u>

O. <u>What OPPORTUNITY do I see to live out this scripture?</u>

E. How can I EXPRESS myself with this scripture?

R. How can I RECOGNIZE this scripture in others?

Proverbs 11:28
Those who trust in riches will be ruined,
but a good person will be healthy like a green leaf.

How can I be S.A.L.T. in my public life?

S. How can I SHOW others?

A. How can I ACKNOWLEDGE this scripture in the actions of others?

L. What can I LISTEN for during conversation?

T. What can I TELL others about this scripture?

Proverbs 11:28
*Those who trust in riches will be ruined,
but a good person will be healthy like a green leaf.*

How can I be a D.O.E.R. in my private life?

D. <u>What can I DO to live out this scripture?</u>

O. <u>What OPPORTUNITY do I see to live out this scripture?</u>

D.O.E.R. 48

E. How can I EXPRESS myself with this scripture?

R. How can I RECOGNIZE this scripture in others?

Stay In Touch

We're thrilled to walk this devotional journey with you! Stay connected and inspired by following us on **Instagram**.

Follow us: @saltanddoer

On our Instagram page, you'll find:

Daily Encouragement: Bite-sized devotionals and scripture reminders.

Community Highlights: Stories and testimonials from our growing family of readers.

Interactive Content: Polls, Q&A, and prayer requests to keep the conversation flowing.

Exclusive Updates: Be the first to know about new releases and events.

Questions or Feedback?
We'd love to hear from you! Send us a message on Instagram at:

@saltanddoer

Let's grow together in faith and purpose!

Made in the USA
Las Vegas, NV
28 November 2025

0bf3881f-8a64-4bfe-a43f-53ebdc90a1f9R01